9/21/22

MAUREEN!

LESSON #99

⊲.⋀

SIX-WORD LESSONS FOR
MIDDLE MANAGERS

100 Lessons Learned
from the Field

Nick D. Anderson

Published by Pacelli Publishing
Bellevue, Washington

Six-Word Lessons for Middle Managers

Cover and interior designed by Pacelli Publishing
Cover art by Tatiana Van Steinburg
Author photo: Pacific Continental Bank

Published by Pacelli Publishing
9905 Lake Washington Blvd. NE, #D-103
Bellevue, Washington 98004
PacelliPublishing.com

ISBN 10: 1-933750-90-1
ISBN-13: 978-1-933750-90-3

Dedication

As I reflect on my own personal experience with leadership, I remember my friend Bill.

Bill Robinson was an imposing figure in most settings, not just for his large frame or his loud and full-of-life voice--and not just because he was the best-dressed man everywhere we went.

Bill always knew people wherever he was, really *knew* them; knew their names and significant upcoming life events and their personal history.

He was imposing because he was so authentic it made the average person uncomfortable.

Bill was a mentor to me. He was a friend. Bill taught leadership. I studied leadership.

Bill delivered his leadership sermon to many, and it always included a gregarious and unyielding statement that, "Leadership is a **CHOICE**!" He would exclaim this, "**Leadership** is a **CHOICE**!" three times. "**Leadership is a CHOICE!**"

I believe you, Bill. Leadership is a choice. I used to think that leadership was my choice, as a wannabe leader. That I could somehow choose to be a leader and that people would follow. I was *almost* right ~ I *almost* understood.

Bill died too early. He was way too young to leave this earth. He left many behind who loved him dearly. I loved him dearly.

His memorial service was attended by hundreds and there were hundreds more, like me, who could not attend. His memory and legacy live on. The positive impact he made on so many lives will ripple through generations.

Bill had cancer. He told only a few. He carried himself every day with pride and dignity and happiness and love and vision and optimism and humanity and clarity and conviction and faith and, and, and. Never with sorrow nor despair nor pity nor failure.

You see, Bill chose to live his life as a leader. Leadership was *his* choice.
And I followed Bill. Bill Robinson informed my life immensely. He told me what he thought I was capable of and I believed him.

I achieved more than I thought I could because I believed in Bill's belief in me.

Leadership was *my* choice. In this case my choice was not to lead, instead my choice was to follow. And so there it was... I then had full and complete understanding: Leadership is a choice.

Leadership is the choice of a person to follow another. To allow themselves to be influenced by another. So much goes into this. Trust. Vulnerability. Belief.

Leadership is the choice of the *follower*.

Leadership is the choice of every individual in that we choose how to live and in so doing, we must acknowledge the potential that others who are watching may choose to follow us. Therefore, I suppose we should be certain that we are living in a way that we want the world to mirror.

Not necessarily always the choice of the leader, but certainly always the choice of those who follow.

Leadership is surely a choice.

Contents

Introduction

Hello, I'm Nick. My corporate career spans 25 years and covers a lot of ground. My LinkedIn profile will show you those details.

What LinkedIn won't reveal is the years invested in my personal growth as a leader and the concurrent years invested in growing others. I have led teams and I have led leaders of teams. Some have been in the same office while others have been across state lines.

I know what it takes to be successful as a middle manager in corporate America. Much of a person's success in corporate America relies on their ability to perform as an individual *and* their perceived leadership potential. My lived experience has proved leadership is a choice--and not the choice of the leader, but rather the choice of another person to follow (you) the leader.

I've helped many professionals grow in their career, make more money, earn titles and promotions--and most importantly to me, the people whom I have served have felt good about their role in the process, and their outcome.

The unique role of a middle manager today requires one to be aware of the needs of many constituents and stakeholders. One might be responsible for a team or a division, or multiple groups with direct reports. Additionally, the individual may be responsible to an executive or multiple executives, perhaps even the CEO. What's more, the middle manager will have peers to whom they are accountable, and the teams they are responsible for also work with peers whom they must rely on. Let's not forget customers, one more group of stakeholders the middle manager must be concerned with. In such a paradigm, there are myriad challenges.

Within this book you will find many of the lessons learned as I tried, failed, learned and succeeded in my own 25-year career.

My perspectives are informed by the philosophies of servant leadership and the desire to create a best-in-class, winning culture. Above all, my intent is to lead myself and my work in a way that glorifies and honors God.

Thanks for reading.

Nick

Leadership Is Always, Always a Choice

Why People Choose to Follow You

Think of the people whom you have followed in your life. Why did you choose to follow them? Was it because you trusted them? Because you admired them? You wanted something they had? These are all reasons one person may choose to follow another, and there are many more. Now-- think to yourself--why would you want someone to choose to follow you? Is it because you live out the ideals of integrity and success? How do you choose to lead?

The Personal Choices You Make Matter

At some point along the way there was a fallacy, a make-believe story, that a person could behave one way "at work" and a completely different way "in real life." Here's the thing: people see right through that. Those who have chosen to follow you will observe everything about your life, the stories you tell and the way you live. Live a life you are proud of!

Without Choice It's Dictating, not Leading

As a manager, you might get people to do what you tell them to do, but what happens when you are not there to tell them? If people choose to follow because they believe in the vision and mission of the work they are doing with you, they will not need to be micromanaged. They may need some assistance solving problems and operating more efficiently, but they will not need you to always tell them what to do.

4

Leaders Don't Need to Go First

If someone on your team is more skilled, more capable, or more ready, get out of their way. If you are the most skilled for an assignment, then you must go first. Just do not confuse the two. If someone is more skilled than you, choose them to do what they do best while you take on a supporting role.

Choose Your Work and People Carefully

If you are going to spend time working on a project, in a team, etc., make sure the work is significant to you, and that you care for the people you are engaging with. Sure, there will be trying times and moments where self-discipline is needed in the absence of motivation, but on the whole, you will always be best served by doing work you can love with people you can love (See Lesson 53).

6

Today's Small Choices Are Tomorrow's Results

If the age-old saying, "Rome wasn't built in a day" described your life right now, what foundation are you laying for the future? Each building block, every small decision you choose to make, will manifest outcomes. This includes the standards and expectations you set for your team as well as the relationships you build with peers. Are you building your own "Rome" in such a way that your future self will be proud?

You Will Be Chosen Without Knowing

Think of everyone who influences you. Do they all know it? Does every person you follow know that you are following them? Of course not. The same is true of others following you. There might be something you do, something you say or an attitude you carry that others admire and want to emulate. There may even be people in other areas of your company who want to work on your team simply because you lead the way you do.

Seek Congruence in Everything You Do

An example of noncongruence: You are on a date, and you are nice to your companion, but rude to the wait staff. Guess what? Your companion will likely think you are rude (because you were) and you might be clueless about it. In a similar manner, your team will observe you interact with peers and your boss. They expect congruence. If you are aggressive with your team and apathetic with your boss, your team will lose trust in you.

Words and Actions Must Be Aligned

One of the areas that trips up many managers is that they somehow believe that, "Do as I say, not as I do," is a good philosophy for leadership. If you wouldn't choose to take an action, why should they? The manager who says he expects team members to be polite with one another, but behaves in a way that is disrespectful to his peers, is jeopardizing credibility and trust with his team.

Trust Is the Most Important Thing

People will follow people they trust. Do what you say and say what you do. Being congruent in all things wherever possible is the way. When your team faces challenges such as tight deadlines or extra hours, you will get the most from a team who trusts you. The same is true for your peers and your boss--their trust in you might just be the make-or-break factor in your success.

The Critical Importance of Making Agreements

Communicate More than You Want To

"I've told them three times already." So what? Maybe they need to hear it six times. Is it more important that you say things less often, or that your team and peers have full and complete understanding of your expectations? If you are behind or facing challenges, tell those who can help you early and often. Do not hide things from bosses either... they will find out. Communicate more.

Seek Confirmation of Their Precise Understanding

Just because you said it, does not mean they understand it. Have them say it back to you. Ask them questions to confirm their understanding. Circle back in a day to re-confirm understanding. Do it early and often because when it's too late, it's too late. More of your success depends on whether those around you understand the assignment than just about anything else.

Pick up the Phone and Call

Years ago, I implemented a three-email rule: If I was replying to the same question a third time via email I chose to pick up the phone and call. It is far more efficient. An issue or opportunity was not being communicated properly that needed dialogue, tone inflection, and/or the observation of nuanced speech to really be understood. Conversation is the best way to resolve confusion.

Recap Every Agreement, Sometimes in Writing

The more important the agreement, the more important the need to recap and capture it in writing. If you have a hard conversation with a team member or peer, follow up with an email bullet-pointing expectations (yours and theirs). If you have a deadline, say it again at the end of the negotiation and follow up with an email. You will be best served by recapping all important agreements verbally and in writing whenever possible.

Without Clear Agreements, Accountability Won't Exist

The first step is to clarify, without any doubt or room for interpretation, what exactly every party is agreeing to. This can seem tedious, but it is important. If you haven't established clear agreements there will be nothing to hold yourself or your peers and teammates accountable to. Otherwise, you will only have your desired outcome and hope. (See Lesson 97)

A Clean Agreement Is Always Best

No, "If this, then that," kind of hooks. Instead, the agreement should be: "I am doing this, you are doing that." Expect delivery. No hedging. This idea also applies when work needs to be done sequentially, such as; someone needs to complete step one before step two is initiated. In such cases, avoid the word *if*. Example: "You will do step one then I will do step two," versus, "I will do #2 *if* you do #1."

17

Agreements Must Be Voluntarily Accepted, Yes?

Do you see that even in these six words I am asking for agreement? You can disagree--that's healthy and makes room for further clarification and under-standing. I am not talking about nuclear arms negotiations here. I am talking about agreements between teammates, colleagues, direct reports and bosses. If all parties do not volunteer their acceptance, it is not an agreement. It is a directive.

Check in with Your People Often

If you believe saying, "I told them what I wanted last week," is enough, you are taking unnecessary risk. Check in. Probably weekly, sometimes daily. Checking in is not micromanaging, it is helping and supporting. Ask, "Do you have what you need? Are we still clear on the priorities? Has anything changed as you've gotten further in? Tell me what you expect in the next week." It is worth the fifteen minutes.

19

Clean and Clear Agreements Are Necessary

In a clean agreement both parties feel good about the resolution. There is no winner/loser. Instead, the outcome is win-win to whatever degree possible. Both sides might feel like they have sacrificed something in exchange for the agreed-on terms, but that can be healthy. In addition to the fairness of a clean agreement, clarity is equally necessary. If there is any room for misunderstanding, the agreement may not in fact be clean.

Same Vocabulary but Many Different Dictionaries

It would not be astonishing to have five people agree they know what the words "hard work" mean. But if each person were asked to write their definition and give an example, there might be five variations of the definition and likely five entirely different examples. Yet we often think we have agreement with people because we have used the same words. Words are important. Meaning is important. The two are not the same.

Vulnerability Versus Insecurity and Trusting Oneself

Vulnerability Is Necessary for Human Connection

Have you ever been in a conversation with someone you just did not connect with? Someone whom you had a hard time believing or trusting? Chances are high they were holding something back or not revealing the truth of their intents and desires. People can sense these things and the only way to achieve a real connection is to share what is important to you in a given situation.

Vulnerability without Security Is Very Dangerous

Before you share what is important to you--your hopes and desires for a given situation--you must be secure in yourself. If you need to ask a peer for support in a challenging project when you are insecure, you risk giving too much in return or feeling inadequate in asking for help. If you ask your boss for a raise or a promotion when you are insecure, you risk taking their response personally and harboring resentment.

Trust the Face in the Mirror

While trust is likely the most important element in the relationships with your team, peers and boss, it is also the most important part of your relationship with yourself. There will be many times you have to make a decision in isolation, by yourself. Do you trust the decision you will make? There will be times you will have to decide between options where one choice benefits you most and the other benefits your team most. What will you do?

24

Safe to Say
I Don't Know

Your demonstration of humility will encourage your team to reciprocate. The very worst cultures are those of fear and judgment, in which people are openly chastised for their shortcomings. If someone on your team is not qualified for the job, you need to have a very specific conversation. Presuming they are qualified, make it okay for them to grow by showing how you learn new things and add skills yourself.

Care What Others Think, a Little

It is sociopathic to not give a rip about what others think of you. And it is debilitating when others' opinions of you are all you consider. The best advice I have to give on this topic is that you should disregard fawning accolades, listen to the critics and block the trolls. Listen to the voices in the middle.

Accept Feedback with Grace and Gratitude

Irrespective of whether feedback is positive or negative, accept it with grace. Caveat: If someone is being abusive, cut it off and walk away. Otherwise, give thanks to those willing to share information that might help you grow and get better. This doesn't mean you have to act on every bit of feedback, but gathering as much data as possible will encourage people to share with you.

Make Every Place
a Safe Space

Listen, things will be difficult. Letdowns and losses inevitably occur. Do not let negative events undermine a healthy culture. You might need to let someone go due to inadequate performance. Do not let these hard times create a culture of insecurity. Be clear in your communication and be clean in your decision-making. If you have put in the work to be transparent about expectations and consequences, people will get it.

Work Harder on Yourself than Them

The coveted peaceful garden of security, self-respect and contentment is just on the other side of that huge mountain called "work." The real work in this case is the work you do on, and for, yourself. The work you put into lifelong learning. The work you put into living a healthy lifestyle. The work you put into showing up in relationships with integrity. These make up the real work.

Allow People around You to Help

There is no such thing as a self-made success. All along the way people have helped, whether you see it or not. An African proverb says, "If you want to go fast, go alone. If you want to go far, go together." Even then, the illusion of going fast alone discounts all the help you received to get to the place of being able to do that. Do not deny yourself the opportunity to go far and do not deny those around you the opportunity to help.

Know Your Values, Set Clear Boundaries

Malcolm X said, "A man who stands for nothing will fall for anything." There will be times in your career when you need to take a stand. Whether the stand you take is for an idea, a teammate, a customer, or a peer--there will be such times. These are defining moments and should be acted upon with the clarity of your personal values. Values that you will not sacrifice.

Leading Up, Down and All Around

Carry the Torch
Like It's Yours

An important reality to accept is this: When you are working in middle management you will have to represent a lot of ideas that are not your own. Doing so with authority and conviction is a difference-maker. Think of it this way: You will contribute ideas to the company that need to be carried out by others. Respect others' ideas as you would have them value yours.

Get the Team What They Need

This might be one of the most important roles of a manager--to get resources to their team as quickly as possible with as little friction as possible. If Erin needs more supplies in order to fulfill customer orders, get them to her. If Dan needs additional temporary employees to meet a deadline, give them to him. If Shantel needs faster tech to handle her workload, make it happen.

Your Boss's Priorities are Your Job

This one may ruffle feathers, but it is simply true. When you are hired for a position, it is because the person who hired you thinks you can help them achieve the priorities set by or for them. You will want to understand what makes your boss successful and contribute to that success.

Six-Word Lessons for Middle Managers

34

Speaking Truth to Power Requires Nuance

The title character in the film, *Jerry Maguire* wrote his manifesto and shared it with the whole company, which lost him his job. I think Jerry's message was right. But, he took a big risk and unless that is your path, there is another way. Dropping a "reply all" email in the middle of the night is not the way. Instead, ask for a discreet one-on-one meeting and deliver truth in a spirit of optimism and genuine compassion.

51

The Golden Rule Works Here Too

If the rule says to treat others as you would have them treat you, we can extrapolate the many benefits of its application to the middle manager's way of leading. Do not ask the team to do anything you would not be willing to do yourself. Treat others the way you want to be treated. Hold yourself to the same level of expectation and accountability.

Your Team Sees All Your Interactions

This speaks to congruence. If you are always nicey-nice with your team and bad-talking others, a breakdown of trust will begin. The same is true in reverse, if you show up acting like Mr. Nice Guy with everyone in the board room but act tyrannical with your team, you will not only lose the team, but your peers will not trust you either. In other words, neither sucking up to the boss or trash-talking peers works. Stay consistent.

37

Own Your Mistakes; Nobody Else Can

Some have been convinced that making mistakes is the worst possible thing that could be done in the workplace. I challenge you to think of it this way: If someone on your team made a mistake, what would you prefer they do? Blame someone else? Hide it? Of course not. Set the example for your team. Be the example for your peers. Show up with your boss the way you expect your team to show up with you. It will be okay.

Be Generous; It Will Come Back

As a middle manager you will rely on those who report to you, those who are adjacent to you on the org chart, support groups, other divisions and sometimes multiple executive-level managers. The more you do to help all the people around you, the more opportunity you will have to receive generosity from them, and often it will come at just the right time.

Be about Results, Always about Results

There are managers who value the time punched in and out over anything else. Some managers value results over anything else. I am a fan of the latter for this reason: The bottom line on any Profit & Loss report does not tell the story of how the company got there, just as a golfer's scorecard does not tell the number of sand traps they hit into. At the end of the game, it is only the score that matters. Ethical behavior is implied.

Consistency Is Predictable, Predictable Is Good

Consistency and predictability are not boring characteristics, they signal reliability. People who depend on you want to know what to expect and what they can count on. Some think that being unpredictable "keeps people on their toes" and they are right about that, however, operating that way does not yield good outcomes. Deliver consistent accountability.

Create Building Blocks and Remove Roadblocks

Leaders Must Quickly Remove the Roadblocks

Removing roadblocks is one of the top functions a leader must be able to perform. The leader will get first-hand reports from the field about what is working and what is not (presuming they have healthy and communicative relationships), so when feedback is given to the leader about something that is broken, the leader should be obsessed with removing or fixing that broken "something."

Leaders Use Challenges to Build Teams

Think about a time you were proud of overcoming adversity. What did you learn? How did you grow? Did your confidence improve? You can leverage a challenge your team is facing into a success story like the one you just remembered. Do not be afraid of challenges--instead embrace them and look for opportunities to use the challenges for learning and growth.

Build Others up Whenever You Can

If it is true that a chain is only as strong as its weakest link, do you want *any* weak links? Consider a person on your team who is struggling, but you know they can perform at a higher level. What's the best way to get them to perform at the height of their potential? Lift them up. Show them your confidence and expect them to live up to it. The opposite of this is pushing others down, openly doubting their capabilities, which creates weak links in the chain.

44

Honor the Legacy of Harder Times

Even if new members on the team were not there to experience a past challenge or play a role in the solution, they can learn from history. Those who built the current paradigm should be recognized for their contribution. Holding open dialogue that honors and respects the significant hurdles your organization has overcome will benefit everyone, old and new.

Deal with the Difficult People Quickly

Sometimes dissenters and naysayers are on your team and sometimes they are not. Do not ignore detractors and critics. If someone has a problem with what you or your team are doing, address it. Work it out. Stick to your values. Hold firm boundaries. Be open to feedback. Make clear agreements. It is too risky to have people shouting you down from the cheap seats and more so when they do it in secret. Address it now.

Get Good at Looking around Corners

As the leader you have a responsibility to anticipate what might happen in the future. Some of your time could be devoted to visualizing potential scenarios, then bringing your team in to solve the challenge or create a contingency plan. Other times, you are studying and learning from those who have gone before you and either succeeded or failed. Learn to anticipate.

Manage to the Most Optimistic Outcome

Would you follow a leader who said, "Come with me and life will be mediocre!" No. People will most enthusiastically follow a leader who has a vision for the future that is better than their own. But having that vision is not enough--the expectation that it will be realized is just as important. The little decisions that indicate the leader's confidence will show up when they are obviously managing to the most optimistic outcome.

48

Anticipate and Document the Important Milestones

Many endurance athletes will break down their challenge by identifying mile markers. Do not think by setting the end goal you have identified all there is to do. Setting a mark for 25 percent completion allows you to gauge if you are on track or not and gives your team a more-achievable, short-term objective--an early win to celebrate, or an opportunity to get back on track.

Build a Plane
Easy to Fly

Ideally, your replacement should be able to step into your job/role and take over easily. Certainly this depends on technical prerequisites so think of it this way: It should be easy for someone equally qualified to do what you do. The antithesis is when you have made your job so complicated only you can do it. The good news is that if you work yourself out of a job you will likely be working yourself into a promotion.

Perfection Is the Enemy of Progress

So often projects get late starts or do not start at all because they were not "ready." This is a fallacy. Nothing is ever executed as precisely as it is imagined. Even a seemingly perfect plan is subject to change. Getting started is the hardest part--so do that. Be tolerant of minor changes and mistakes. This will invite team members to push harder and try more. Who knows, maybe the end result will be better than the original plan!

Building Relationships
with Teams
and Colleagues

51

Understand the Difference: Vasopressin Versus Oxytocin

Good times produce oxytocin. Hard times produce the hormone vasopressin. The most difficult times--layoffs, closures, mergers, hostile takeovers, new CEOs, economic recession--these are all scenarios where a team can forge life-long bonds if led properly. Happy hours or bowling ain't gonna have the same effect. Find a middle ground.

When Real Life Happens, Acknowledge It

You and your team will live through all kinds of life events--birth, death, marriage, divorce, cancer, etc. If you want your team to give their all to the work and to each project, you must give it back. Sometimes that means giving space. Sometimes that means giving love.

53

Do not Be Afraid to Love

Agape love is the way here. Agape goes beyond emotions to the extent of seeking the best for others. It is the unconditional love that transcends and persists regardless of circumstance. According to 1 Timothy 1:5 (King James Version), it is love, ". . . out of a pure heart, and of a good conscience, and of faith unfeigned . . ."

54

When You Fall
Who Will Catch?

Imagine attending a team-building workshop and you're asked to perform a trust fall with no one there to catch you. Now, imagine thinking you are the lone wolf, top producer, best in the business and something bad happens. Who will be there to help you? Maybe your team has your back, but your peers despise your arrogance and hubris. Who will have your back in the boardroom when no one from your team is around?

55

They Feel Included When They Are

I listened to an audiobook recently which advised listeners to "make (them) feel included in the process." That's weak sauce. What you should do is actually include them in the process. When you include people they will "feel" included, because they are included. Anything else is manipulative.

Managing Peer Relationships Is Important Work

Your peer relationships are critical to your team's success. You might rely on another department to fulfill your sales orders or deliver quality product on time for your team's customers. In a pinch, you want your peers to *want* to help you because you have formed good relationships. Keep in mind that people talk with one another, so always protect your reputation.

Be a Real Person with Everyone

The thing about authenticity is that, as an idea, it is way overused. And the thing about authenticity, as a practice, is that it is rarely used enough. Authenticity does not mean showing all your cards, all the time. It does not give you a free pass to express all your emotions in every circumstance. What it does mean is that you should not behave like someone you are not to win approval.

Listen Much More than You Speak

The saying goes, "God gave us two ears and one mouth." If that is not enough to understand the idea, we can acknowledge that it is impossible to really listen while you are talking. Keep this in mind: The goal is not to be heard—the goal is to be understood. How can you improve your chances of being understood? By understanding who you are talking to and their ideas.

Trust Is Earned through Consistent Response

Imagine this: You go to your boss one day and say, "How many widgets do we need to make this week?" and the response is "10." Next week your team makes 10 widgets, and your boss says, "10 widgets is not enough, your team needs to make at least 12." Will you trust your boss the next time you ask a question? Will you feel secure in your performance if the team makes 12 widgets? Do not be that boss.

Make Virtual Communication like Hallway Conversation

When working remotely you are likely to miss out on the small-talk opportunities that come up in a workplace environment. So, pick up the phone once in a while and touch base for no reason. Call (do not email) a peer colleague to connect on a personal level. It does not have to be a scheduled hour-long meeting, just an impromptu call every now and again. It will go a long way toward developing and maintaining relationships.

Roles and Assignments Must Be Clear

Know Everyone's Role, Especially Your Own

Imagine a football team on the field with the center standing behind the quarterback. Or an operating room where the radiologist asks a nurse for a scalpel. These things do not make sense, right? Who answers incoming emails for product information requests? Who is responsible for quality control? Make sure these roles and responsibilities are clearly defined, including your own role in the process.

Round Pegs Fit in Square Holes

If someone is not the right fit for the job it might be that they represent a round peg, and the role is square-shaped, leaving room for growth. (Imagine a circle drawn inside a square--fill the corners with growth.) The harder challenge is fitting the square peg in the round hole (refer to the same image). To make it fit you need to shave off the corners--a challenge not many are ready for. Find the round peg for the square hole. Leave room for growth.

See the Goal, Communicate the Vision

To say to your team or your colleagues, "We are going to make a thousand widgets this year!" does not have the same impact as saying, "We are going to have our most successful year of production ever and each one of you will grow to new levels of success in your career! To do that, we need to make a thousand widgets."

People Will Believe in Your Belief

There have been many, many times I have questioned myself. Very often I would ask my bosses for their opinion even when I knew the answer, because I was insecure. During those times when I worked for exceptional leaders I not only got the answer to my questions, but I was also encouraged to believe in my capabilities, because my bosses believed in me.

Stay in Your Lane Most Often

We often hear the expression, "Stay in your lane." But how are you ever going to learn a new skill, or grow if you do? You have got to first be willing, then able, to change lanes when necessary. This means you must get comfortable with someone coming into your lane, too. Refer to the next lesson on boundaries.

Be Clear about What You Accept

Setting clear expectations and making your boundaries known up-front and often will make it easier for your team, your colleagues and your leadership to know how to engage with you. There is nuance to this. You must not be too rigid and tight with boundaries, or you will limit yourself and the collective opportunity. Likewise, you must not be so loose that you get overrun, overlooked or devalued.

Commit to Success and the Process

Clarifying roles and assignments implies some level of tactical clarity. Not only does every person need to know their role and assignment, but they should also know the roles and assignments of their teammates, especially those with whom they work closely. With this clarity, you can ask for commitment to a shared vision of success and more importantly, commitment to the process by which success is to be achieved.

Make the Plan Simple, Stay Committed

Complex plans with myriad details are more likely to be disrupted than simple, straightforward plans. When there are more levers to pull, more levers will get pulled. Imagine you are halfway into your project and you have 15 key variables identified. Which do you adjust? What are the implications of changing two or three to the overall outcome? Too complex. Keep it simple and stick to the plan, unless you are convinced it will fail.

If Failure Is Certain, Change Direction

In what seems like a contradiction to the prior lesson, don't allow yourself to stay committed to a failing plan. If your plan was simple, you have stayed the course, and you have identified clear benchmarks for performance, you will know if you are on track or not. Dismiss the fallacy that there is a point of no return. Become the Phoenix risen from the ashes.

Measure Performance with Clear Objective Benchmarks

In baseball, batters hitting third in the batting order are expected to advance runners already on base and try to get on base themselves. This is an example of good role and assignment clarity. If the batter does not get on base and advance runners, he will be moved to a less critical batting order position. When employees are not meeting role and assignment expectations, consider changing roles and positions to better align with expectations.

Conflicts Will Happen, Deal with Them

Conflicts Left Unaddressed will Fester Uncontrollably

You cannot simply ignore problems on your team. Just like you cannot ignore challenges stemming from other departments with which you interact. Despite this being true, avoidance is a surprisingly common response to conflict. First, get yourself in a mental and emotional place in which you feel secure and then address the conflict. It has to happen sometime, so do not put it off for too long.

Your Goal Is Making Clean Agreements

See Lesson 19 defining clean agreements. Whenever there is conflict, it is possible the root issue is beyond reconciliation. You can't always choose who you work alongside, and people in more senior roles or other divisions can have considerable influence on your reputation and career. The goal should not be to make friends at all costs. With difficult colleagues, it is better to make clear and clean agreements.

Wake up Proud in the Morning

Heated arguments and distasteful behavior can occur in the workplace just like anywhere else. Things might be said to and about people that are inappropriate, or worse. In times of conflict emotions run high. It is a double-whammy to wake up the next day with the aftertaste of regret for something that was said the day before.

Always Remember that Change Is Hard

It it is useful to acknowledge that change impacts people differently and when factors line up in certain ways, circumstances can be overwhelming. At a minimum, people will not adapt to, or adopt, a new "thing" at the same pace. Focus on the early adopters to move the team forward, as well as the hesitant ones holding others back. You will have to work with all of them at some point. Can the early adopters bring the hesitant along?

Focus on Solutions not the Person

Be known as the leader who is committed to solutions and not interpersonal gamesmanship. Sometimes, solutions require relenting; other times solutions require assertion. Take the focus off of differences in personalities. Solutions should never merit one's personal gain and another's loss as in, "I win, you lose." If your teammate, colleague or leader loses, so do you.

If You're Right, Why Prove It?

Sometimes you just gotta let stuff go. If you know a situation or outcome is good, and you know it is right, why fight over a small "win" just to prove a point, or have the final word? Even when the best result is eventually achieved, the collective impact to the team of not letting go might be damaging.

Seek First to Understand the Problem

Get good at asking questions when you have conflict. Try to understand another's point of view with a request such as, "Please help me understand the way you are seeing this issue and what might be done to resolve it." If you have a technical problem, say, "Can you help me see where we might have missed something, or if there is another way to approach this issue?" Or, my favorite, "Have we properly identified the problem here?"

Clarify and Define Everything You Can

Conflict is most prevalent when there is miscommunication or misunderstanding. Either you have not said what you wanted to say very well, or you haven't understood what others are trying to say to you. These situations are certainly reversible. Conflict resolution often begins with basic clarification of objectives, intentions, and expectations. Seems tedious. Worth the effort.

People Are Good; Remember these Words

The moment you start thinking the "other side" is bad, or has something against you, is the moment you lose. Many times when you are in an argument, you still lose when you win because relationships are damaged. Just like you are a good person who has bad days, give others the same grace and understanding.

It's Always Important to Look Within

Listen, I know people will do things that are offensive or just plain wrong. But conflict doesn't often result from an individual doing something independently of any other consideration. Can you securely look at your own contribution to whatever is happening? Can you accept that you might have added fuel to a fire?

Growth Is the Only Way Up

81

Anticipation: The Superpower of Experienced Leaders

Just as you have evolved, so will any given situation. What do you know about potential pitfalls, competitors, and operational challenges? Draw on your past experiences to predict what might happen and plan for it. Breadth and depth of experiences are key factors here.

Slow Down to Speed It Up

External pressures are real. Stakeholders need you to deliver accurate and timely products or services. Deadlines are looming. People are counting on you. Taking a break may seem like the last thing you should do, but it often is not. In times of high anxiety, taking a break and slowing down can actually enhance productivity. Consider this: Will 15 minutes threaten your deadline, really? Take a walk and process what is going on.

Regularly Investigate and Calibrate Your Intuition

"Go with your gut" can be the very best and the very worst advice ever. If your intuition is off and you follow it, you will be lost. Look at your life and professional experiences objectively. Has your intuition always been correct? When have you listened to your intuition and regretted it? Use this information to recalibrate your "gut instinct."

Look for Opportunities that Are Uncomfortable

This is where growth happens and you learn about yourself. Do I like this? Is this something I can grow into? Can I excel in this new area? The same is true for providing opportunities for your team and your colleagues--and the more you can walk alongside them, the better.

85

Define the Process, Refine the Process

Process is not often the first thing to receive attention. When an idea is novel, it may not be as critical to define the processes by which the end product is developed. Once the idea is ready to market, it becomes critical to organize and define processes to improve efficiencies. As processes are implemented and tested, use feedback from your team and the market to continually refine for maximum utility.

Audit Your Process Over and Over

After you have observed, tested and refined your process, you will be well served to continue auditing the process frequently as market demands change or as human or technological resource availabilities shift. What may have been the most efficient, highest quality process yesterday might not be the same tomorrow.

87

What You Were, You Are Not

Visualize this idea by thinking of a typically developing baby who cannot talk, walk or feed themselves. That baby will grow into an adult who will be able to perform these functions. What then leads you to believe that the skills you have today cannot be complemented and further developed to help you become a more effective leader? Consider the same for your teammates and peers. We all will be someone different a year from now.

If You're not Growing, You're Dying

I heard this once when I was a young professional and it never left me: "The moment we are born we start growing. That lasts a few decades and then our bodies start dying." A little bit sad. But, a person committed to lifelong growth of the heart, the mind and the soul can minimize the regrets of dying by continuing to engage in a full and rewarding life experience.

As You Grow so Will They

Building on the prior lesson, many managers are quick to acknowledge the importance of growth in the people they are responsible for. However, not all are aware of their own need for growth. Set the standard and lead by example, so that as you invest in your own growth, your people will be encouraged to do the same.

90

Discipline Is the Way to Grow.

Growth does not happen because you wish it would. Growth happens when habits are formed, and habits are formed through discipline. Pick any areas in which you would like to grow or improve. Now identify the habits of those who excel in these areas. What will it take for you to emulate those habits? Discipline. You must often take action when you do not want to.

Work + Life Balance.
Is It Possible?

Work to Live, not the Opposite

At some point you will have to accept an inherent truth of being in middle management: You work for someone else. As you acknowledge this, you must also acknowledge it is true for your team members. Choose for yourself--and create a culture for your team--that recognizes there is more to life than the job. This will actually improve performance and results.

Unhealthy Leaders Will have Unhealthy Teams

Leaders who burn the candle at both ends might expect their teams to do the same. Even if they do not set the expectation, they do set the standard. Additionally, leaders who do not value health and fitness will buy doughnuts for every staff meeting. Now apply this principle to integrity, values, and healthy boundaries and you have a very impactful set of considerations to assess regarding the tone you set for your team.

93

The 5-9 Matters More than 9-5

Stephen Covey said, "The main thing is to keep the main thing the main thing." As a leader you must realize whatever work your team is doing involves means to an end. The primary objective of people working on your team is to provide for the life they have outside of work. Other objectives--making a difference and changing the world--might also apply so I encourage you to remember that, by definition, only *one* thing can be *primary*.

94

Discipline Works for Health and Wealth

Self-discipline, saying no and holding boundaries, is the only way to achieve the utopia known as work-life balance. To believe there is a static level of balance that leaves you perfectly content at the end of each workday is ostensible. To be balanced you must have the discipline to work when you do not want to and say no to work when you should. Put in the hours late one night so you can be free for weekend plans with friends and family.

Work Is a Four-Letter Word

It is ironic that I would say this in a book written supporting the nobility of work, but let's face it, if we did not need the money, would anyone "work?" I do not think so. I believe many would volunteer, create, build, exercise, etc., but would that really be "work"? Often the people on your team are working because they have to, not because they want to. Stay humble.

96

Manage to the Optimistic, with Hedges

Like a stop-loss in trading protects an investment from the downside, you will serve your team, company and yourself by having backup plans. However, you cannot be successful by setting a strategy that relies on the backup plan as its primary objective. You must pick the best, most realistic outcome and go for it earnestly.

Hope Is not a Winning Strategy

Hope is a mindset and it's a good one to have. However, hope cannot be the only tool in the shed. Hope drives. Hope can provide the energy behind a strategy. Yet, hope cannot be the only thing. Due diligence and operational assessments are needed, as are tactical and market assessments. Strategy is thoughtful and detailed whereas hope does not have to be. Hope can be naive while strategy must be informed.

98

Remember Why You Do this Work

Simon Sinek nailed it in his book, *Start With Why* as he gave the world a fresh perspective that few understood at the time. Discovering your "why" and reminding yourself of that "why" are two different endeavors. The discovery can be painful or joyful as you travel the journey of life. Remembering why takes discipline and might require a picture on your desk, an alarm, or multiple recurring calendar reminders.

99

An Intentional Life Has no Mistakes

This is an ambitious statement, but roll with me. We will all experience turbulence in our lives. This is an immutable fact. Unplanned events will occur and often you will wish they didn't. But listen, if you are living intentionally, even if you swerve a little along the way, you are unlikely to go completely off the road. Make sense?

In the End
Give It Everything

"Send it" is the motto of the day. Standing at the bottom of the hill, looking at the daunting tasks ahead of you, choose to put all you've got into what you do. Some would simply say, "Anything worth doing is worth doing right." So, go do it right. And if you have decided you cannot give everything to what you have in front of you--do it anyway, one last time--and then find something else to do.

From the Author

I hope you have enjoyed reading this book as much as I enjoyed writing it!

To distill twenty-five years of experience down to one-hundred lessons was a challenging task. It is work I'm grateful to have the opportunity to share.

As you embark on, or continue your journey of leadership and influence through your work, do so knowing that perfection is impossible, whereas sincere effort with humility and integrity are all that anyone wants from you.

I'd like to thank the Pacellis for their encouragement and support throughout the process, they truly are delightful partners!

With honor and glory to God,

Nick

References

Jerry Maguire. Directed, written and produced by Cameron Crowe, starring Tom Cruise, 1996.

Stephen R. Covey, *The 7 Habits of Highly Effective People* (New York: Simon & Schuster, 1989, 2004, 2020.)

Simon Sinek, *Start With Why: How Great Leaders Inspire Everyone to Take Action* (New York: Penguin Books, 2009)

About the Six-Word Lessons Series

Legend has it that Ernest Hemingway was challenged to write a story using only six words. He responded with the story, "For sale: baby shoes, never worn." The story tickles the imagination. Why were the shoes never worn? The answers are left up to the reader's imagination.

This style of writing has a number of aliases: postcard fiction, flash fiction, and micro-fiction. Lonnie Pacelli was introduced to this concept in 2009 by a friend, and started thinking about how this extreme brevity could apply to today's communication culture of text messages, tweets and Facebook posts. He wrote the first book, *Six-Word Lessons for Project Managers*, then he and his wife Patty started helping other authors write and publish their own books in the series.

The books all have six-word chapters with six-word lesson titles, each followed by a one-page description. They can be written by entrepreneurs who want to promote their businesses, or anyone with a message to share.

See the entire *Six-Word Lessons Series*
at **6wordlessons.com**